RICHMOND HILL
PUBLIC LIBRARY

SEP 0 3 2013

CENTRAL LIBRARY
905-884-9288

BOOK
NO LONGER

D1172405

RED & WHITE
WINE

RED & WHITE
WINE

How to choose, taste & enjoy it

Jonathan Ray

photography by Alan Williams

LONDON • NEW YORK

For David, Jamie and Tom

Designer Sarah Rock

Editor Henrietta Heald

Production Manager
Gordana Simakovic

Art Director Leslie Harrington

Editorial Director Julia Charles

First published as two books, *Red Wine*
and *White Wine,* in 2001 and 2008
This combined and updated edition
first published in 2013
by Ryland Peters & Small
20–21 Jockey's Fields
London WC1R 4BW
and
519 Broadway, 5th Floor
New York, NY 10012
www.rylandpeters.com
10 9 8 7 6 5 4 3 2 1

Text © Jonathan Ray 2001, 2008, 2013
Design and photographs copyright
© Ryland Peters & Small 2001, 2008, 2013
except photographs on pages 24, 28, 35,
38, 56, 58, 60, 74, 85, 87 and 96 copyright
© Alan Williams

The author's moral rights have been
asserted. All rights reserved. No part
of this publication may be reproduced,
stored in a retrieval system, or
transmitted in any form or by any means,
electronic, mechanical, photocopying or
otherwise, without the prior permission
of the publisher.

ISBN: 978-1-84975-363-0

A CIP record for this book is available
from the British Library and from the
Library of Congress.

Printed in China.

RICHMOND HILL
PUBLIC LIBRARY

SEP 03 2013

CENTRAL LIBRARY
905-884-9288

Contents

Introduction

As a subject, wine can seem daunting at first. I mean, where on earth to start? Well, come on, what better way to start than by opening a bottle and pouring yourself a glass? Swirl it, sniff it and sip it, and work out what you think. What does it taste of? Do you recognise it? Does it remind you of anything? Have you had it before? Does it go with what you're eating? Do you like it or not?

There's really nothing to be afraid of. After all, wine is nothing more than fermented grape juice, made in some sun-dappled vineyard for you and me to enjoy and to relax with, over supper maybe, on holiday or with friends. The key to getting to grips with wine, though, is to know and understand your grape varieties. For while climate, soil, methods of production and the skill and philosophy of the winemaker all make significant contributions to the way a wine tastes, the most important factor by far is the grape itself. Chardonnay, for example, however it's vinified, tastes very different from Muscat, just as Gamay tastes very different from Syrah.

The following pages will introduce you to the world's major red and white grape varieties and explain where they're grown and what wines they make; how to store them, serve them and enjoy them.

Remember though, that this is only the starting point and that there is plenty of accompanying course work required, such as opening that bottle and pouring yourself a glass…

red wine

bottle shapes
& sizes

The regular wine bottle is standardized the world over at 75 cl. Other sizes such as half-bottles (37.5 cl), litre bottles (100 cl) and magnums (150 cl) are also often seen. The general rule of thumb is that the larger the bottle the more slowly the wine within it will mature – and the longer it will keep – owing to the ratio of wine to oxygen in the bottle.

The two main shapes of bottle for red wines are those common to Bordeaux – green with high shoulders – or Burgundy and the Rhône – greeny brown with sloping shoulders.

As a rule, Californian and Australian varietals such as Cabernet Sauvignon and Merlot come in Bordeaux-style bottles, as do Zinfandel, Chianti and some Riojas.

Beaujolais, California Pinot Noir, Italians such as Barolo and Barbaresco, Rhônes, Syrah and some Spanish wines come in Burgundy-style bottles, although such distinctions are becoming blurred.

Port bottles are made of opaque black glass with high shoulders and a long, thick neck.

The larger the bottle the more slowly the wine within it will mature.

Although idiosyncratic designs are now a regular feature of wine bottles, the shape and colour of the bottle are still good – but not official – indications of the wine's origin.

red wine:
labels explained

In essence, wine labels are no different from the labels to be found on cans of baked beans or jars of coffee. They are there to give you all the information you need to make an informed decision about whether or not to buy the product.

Among the items of information that must, by law, appear on a label on the front or back of a bottle are:

- the wine's name
- the size of the bottle
- the vintage (if there is one)
- the wine's alcoholic strength
- the producer's name and address
- the name of the bottler (if different from the producer)
- the name of the importer
- the name of the shipper (if different from the importer)
- the wine's quality level
- whether the wine contains sulphites
- where the wine was bottled
- the wine's country of origin
- the wine's region and appellation (if relevant)

Some labels also include the grape variety.

Most countries now insist on displaying on their wine bottles a government health warning about the hazards of drinking wine (with not a word about the proven benefits). Wines sold in the USA, for example, must show stern admonitions about the perils of alcohol from the Surgeon General, while those sold in France caution pregant women not to drink.

The statement *mis(e) en bouteille(s) au château* on a bottle of French wine indicates that the wine was bottled at the property where it was made.

As a rule, New World producers market their wines by grape variety, while the Europeans tend not to (although this is changing), so it helps to know which varieties make which wines.

While front labels are strictly regulated, (optional) back labels often give a fuller explanation of the wine. They might tell you which foods go well with the wine, how long it should be kept, when it should be opened, what temperature it should be served at, and so on. Neck labels are sometimes added, stating the vintage or some special feature of the wine, or displaying an award won.

red wine: single varietals & blends

A blended wine is a wine in which the fermented juice of one variety of grape is joined or co-fermented with that of another – or others, as happens in Bordeaux, where any claret might be a blend of up to five different varieties, or in Australia, say, where it is commonplace to blend Cabernet Sauvignon with Shiraz.

Blending can also encompass different vintages, as in ports or standard house clarets, blended in a way that ensures that they always taste the same.

Strictly speaking, a single varietal is a wine made from one grape variety only. However, rules differ from region to region and, in truth, a single varietal might contain a small amount of another variety. For example, in Australia 80 per cent of the wine must come from the named variety, while in the USA it is 75 per cent.

It used to be the case that most New World wines were single varietals while most from the Old World were blends, but this distinction has now become blurred. What remains true is that some producers prefer the purity and intensity of single varietals while others think that careful blending leads to greater subtlety and delicacy.

In Europe the trend has been to name the wines after the place of origin rather than after the variety. This is where some knowledge is useful. For example, if you know that you like single-varietal Pinot Noirs from Oregon, say, it is helpful to know that all red burgundies, such as Vosne-Romanée, Pommard and Aloxe Corton, are also single varietals, being 100 per cent Pinot Noir.

There are strong arguments in favour of blends and of single varietals – arguments that are rehearsed whenever two or more wine makers are gathered together. Neither style is better than the other; they are just different.

cabernet sauvignon

Cabernet Sauvignon is instantly recognizable in the glass owing to its overwhelming aroma of blackcurrants, its juicy, jammy flavours and its structure, tannin levels and complexity. It has the ability to age exceptionally well.

Cabernet Sauvignon is the most important variety in Bordeaux, but it is never used on its own there; claret producers believe that its qualities can only be enhanced by blending it with one or more of the quartet of Cabernet Franc, Malbec, Merlot, Petit Verdot.

Okay, this is the big one! Cabernet Sauvignon is, without doubt, the most cherished red grape variety in the world, acclaimed as the backbone behind the finest clarets of Bordeaux, and producer of the New World's finest single varietals.

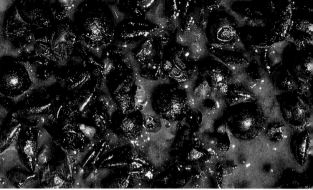

Cabernet Sauvignon is grown throughout Europe. In Italy it is grown in Emilia–Romagna and Piedmont, and is used to great effect in Tuscany, where it kick-started the 'Super Tuscan' revolution. The variety is also becoming more popular in Spain, where it is frequently blended with Tempranillo.

It was Cabernet Sauvignon that first brought California to the attention of the wine world, with the best examples usually coming from the Napa Valley and Sonoma County. Hitherto it has often been made as a single varietal (although many so-called Cabernet Sauvignons include tiny amounts of Merlot, Cabernet Franc, Petit Verdot or Malbec), but producers have recently been

moving away from single varietals towards making so-called Meritage blends, similar in style to Bordeaux, and insisting on using French oak too. Some producers even use Cabernet Sauvignon to make fortified, port-style wines.

In Australia, Cabernet Sauvignon has an even more pronounced aroma of blackcurrants and is often blended with Shiraz or Merlot; Coonawarra in South Australia is the most favoured spot in the country for growing the variety. Chile makes some of the finest and best value Cabernet Sauvignons (from pre-phylloxera vines), which are exquisitely dark and intense with extraordinary depth. Other examples of increasing finesse are found in New Zealand and South Africa.

Cabernet Sauvignon in all its forms goes well with roast meats, steaks, game and most cheeses.

merlot

In the Médoc area of Bordeaux, Merlot is most definitely the junior partner to Cabernet Sauvignon's chairman of the board, being used in blends to soften the latter's dominance. On the right bank of the river Garonne however, in St Émilion, Pomerol, Fronsac, Bourg and Blaye, it plays by far the greater role.

Merlot is increasingly being grown in Languedoc-Roussillon. It is an important grape in north-east Italy, especially in Friuli, Emilia-Romagna, Trentino-Alto Adige and the Veneto, and is often a component of the 'Super Tuscans', being blended with Sangiovese and Cabernet Sauvignon. At its lowest level, however, Italian Merlot can be unwelcomingly thin and light-bodied with very high acidity.

In the New World, unblended Merlot can make wines of great style. It is argued that North America's best Merlot comes from Washington state, but it is increasing in popularity in California too, California Merlots being heavier and fuller than those of Bordeaux. In South America, Argentina makes some very good Merlots in Tupungato, Mendoza and those of Chile are especially silky and elegant, although they tend not to age quite so well.

Even though many people used to believe that New Zealand was only suited to making white wine, Merlot is a big success in the country, especially in Hawkes Bay. Plantings are limited in Australia, where producers and consumers seem to prefer Shiraz for single varietals or Cabernet Sauvignon for blends.

Merlot is grown more or less everywhere that Cabernet Sauvignon is grown. In Bordeaux, Merlot is a crucial part of the blends that make claret, while in the New World it makes top-quality single varietals.

Merlot from whatever country is ideal with any poultry dishes, simply cooked lamb and soft cheeses.

pinot noir

Pinot Noir has been grown in Burgundy for centuries and – unblended – makes the region's world-famous red wines, including Clos de Vougeot, Pommard, Gevrey-Chambertin, Corton, Beaune, Nuits-St-Georges and Romanée-Conti. It also plays a major part in the wines of Champagne, but that's another story.

Burgundy is reputed to be one of hardest wine regions to fathom, with wines of the same name being made by vast numbers of different growers, producers and *négoçiants*. One thing, however, should make the region easy to understand, and that is that all its red wines (barring the very lowliest, such as Bourgogne Passe-Tout-Grains) are made from one grape and one grape only – Pinot Noir. And while the gap between top-quality and low-quality burgundy is large, nowhere else in the world is the grape so dominant. Some old Pinot Noirs from Burgundy are characterized by a smell of

Red burgundy goes well with Coq au Vin and Boeuf Bourguignon; Alsace Pinot Noir with quiche and onion tart; California or Oregon Pinot Noir with grilled salmon and tuna.

farmyards, but don't let that put you off, because they taste sublime and are highly prized. Pinot Noir does well in the Loire, where it produces the charming red and rosé Sancerres, and in Alsace – a region better-known for aromatic white wines – where the locals lap it up, so much so that it is rarely exported.

Being a famously bad traveller, the Pinot Noir grape has been less triumphant outside France than other classic grape varieties, although superb examples are now being produced in the New World. Unlike Cabernet Sauvignon, which tends to taste just about the same wherever it is grown, Pinot Noir can taste very different in different locations. Oregon, California, Chile, South Africa, the Yarra Valley and Mornington Peninsula in Victoria, Australia, and Martinborough and Central Otago in New Zealand all produce wonderful examples with buckets of raspberry and bitter-cherry flavours.

Syrah's wines are instantly identifiable by oodles of pepper and spice on the nose, combined with plenty of blackberries and plums. Its wines are packed with tannin and so have the ability to age for decades.

syrah

Dominating the northern Rhône in the same way that Grenache dominates the southern Rhône, Syrah is responsible for the production of such famous wines as the full-bodied Cornas, Hermitage and Côte Rôtie, and the slightly lighter Crozes-Hermitage and Saint Joseph.

The grape almost certainly originated in the Middle East and was brought by the Romans to the Rhône Valley, where it continues to produce wines of stunning concentration and full-bodied intensity.

Syrah is an easy grape to grow. It produces a reliable crop, is resistant to most pests and diseases and does especially well in poor soils and warm climates, and so can flourish on the precipitous granite slopes above the river Rhône. Not only does Syrah rule the roost in the northern Rhône, it also plays a small but important part in Grenache territory in the southern Rhône, by adding flavour, weight and body to the wines of Châteauneuf-du-Pape.

Syrah's other great stronghold is Australia, where it first arrived in the 1830s. Since then, known as Shiraz, it has become the country's most widely planted grape. It is either made into lip-smacking blends alongside Cabernet Sauvignon or into long-lived single varietals, the most celebrated example of which is Penfolds Grange – a powerfully intense wine to rival the finest in the world.

Although Syrah has yet to match in North America the success it has enjoyed in France and Australia, it is now being more widely planted in California – either for Rhône-style blends or single varietals. The grape is also flourishing in both South America and South Africa.

Syrah in all its forms goes well with cassoulet and barbecued food, casseroles or roasts. Its spiciness also complements strongly flavoured dishes such as pepperoni pizza.

Cabernet Franc should not be confused with Cabernet Sauvignon, compared to which it is less tannic, less acidic, less full-bodied, but more aromatic – its wines often smelling of blackcurrant leaves. It is a small but significant component in many claret blends, while also being the predominant ingredient in one of the world's great wines – Château Cheval Blanc.

cabernet franc

In the Médoc in Bordeaux, Cabernet Franc is very much the understudy to Cabernet Sauvignon's star turn. It is grown not only to boost the flavour of its near namesake in the claret blends, but also, since it ripens earlier, as its substitute in the event that the lead performer is indisposed by the weather. Cabernet Franc takes a far more prominent role in nearby St Émilion, where most wines are blended from Cabernet Franc and Merlot. Its

performance is also taken more seriously in the Loire, where it enjoys the cool conditions, making early-maturing light red wines such as Chinon, Saumur-Champigny, Bourgeuil and the lovely rosé Cabernet d'Anjou.

Although Cabernet Sauvignon is securely established in California, where the benign climate ensures that it rarely fails, the earlier ripening Cabernet Franc continues to be grown there in sizeable amounts

as a flavour-boosting back-up.
It is also used in the region's
Bordeaux-style Meritage wines,
and there are a few producers
who make single varietals from
it, as there are in Australia.

Cabernet Franc can also be
found in modest amounts in
Argentina, New York state,
Washington state, New Zealand
and in Friuli, in north-eastern
Italy, where, misleadingly, it
is sometimes labelled simply
as Cabernet.

barbera

Barbera thrives in warm to hot climates, producing wines high in fruit and acidity, and low in tannin. One of the most productive varieties in Italy, it is eclipsed in terms of quality if not ubiquity by the grandees Nebbiolo and Sangiovese.

Rather than making great wines, Barbera makes reliable everyday wines that are purple-coloured with good acidity and plenty of chewy, raisiny fruit. Barbera's wines need little time to mature and their low tannin levels ensure that they are softly quaffable and always a pleasure to drink, without ever reaching the heights enjoyed by their two big rivals, Nebbiolo and Sangiovese.

Barbera's main homes are Piedmont, Lombardy and Emilia-Romagna in northern Italy. Its best-known wines are Barbera d'Alba, Barbera d'Asti - both robust and full-bodied - and, in combination with other varieties, Barbera del Monferrato. Very versatile, Barbera is capable of making rosés and sparkling wines, some of which can be sweet. But, despite its undoubted qualities, its popularity appears to be on the wane in Italy - in several areas, it is giving way to other varieties.

Further afield, in hotter regions, Barbera's high alcohol and good acidity levels make it an ideal variety for blending, and there are plantings of it in Argentina, Uruguay, Central Valley in California, Malmesbury and Paarl in South Africa and parts of Slovenia.

Barbera's high natural acidity means that its wines go especially well with rich food, such as dishes with creamy sauces, as well as pasta, cold meats or roasted vegetables.

Carignan was, until recently, France's most widely grown red grape, making dark, hefty wines that are high in alcohol and tannin. It never makes great wine, but nor does it make bad wine either: at its best it is fruity and spicy, at its worst, inoffensive and dull.

carignan (cariñena)

Carignan originated in the Cariñena area of Aragon in northern Spain, where it continues to make fairly dreary full-bodied table wine. Although it is an integral part of the wines of Rioja, adding colour to that region's wines, its main home in Spain is Catalonia, where it is also chiefly used for blending.

Being a late-ripener, Carignan does well in hot climates, and it has long dominated Languedoc-Roussillon, especially in Aude, Hérault, Gard and Pyrénées-Orientales. These days, however, it is no longer in fashion and many of its vines are being uprooted and replanted with more popular varieties.

Although most of its wines end up as simple *vin de table*, Carignan does play an important part in the blends that make up such well-regarded French country wines as Corbières, Fitou, Minervois and the Provençal rosés. Its regular blending partners are Cinsault in the western Midi and Grenache in the eastern Midi.

Carignan is extremely well travelled and continues to be grown in such diverse locations as Algeria, Argentina, California, Chile, Italy, Israel, Mexico and Uruguay. It probably produces more red wine than any other variety, though rarely as a single varietal, which is why its name is less familiar than others.

It is hard to believe, but **Carignan** was once the most widely grown variety in California, until a **gum-chewing** grape called Cabernet Sauvignon hit town . . .

All red Beaujolais, be it the grandest top cru or the humblest Beaujolais Nouveau is made solely from unblended Gamay.

gamay

Although Beaujolais, in the south of Burgundy, is Gamay's main home, the grape is also grown successfully in the Loire, where it makes wines such as Anjou Rosé, Anjou Gamay, and Gamay de Touraine, often referred to – unfairly – as poor man's Beaujolais. Switzerland, too, grows a considerable quantity of Gamay, most frequently blending it with Pinot Noir.

In the Mâconnais and the Côte Chalonnaise in Burgundy, Pinot Noir is also used as Gamay's blending partner in the easy-drinking Bourgogne Passe-Tout-Grains, adding body and depth.

Gamay makes light, fresh, fruity red wines packed with the juicy flavours of peaches, cherries and berries. Typically, its wines are high in acid, low in tannin and sometimes lacking depth, but they are eminently quaffable and are among the few red wines that benefit from being lightly chilled, making them perfect for summer drinking. Gamay is at its best when drunk young, and only the highest quality Beaujolais from fine years should be left to mature.

Posters announcing that *Le Beaujolais Nouveau est arrivé* are a familiar sight in wine bars every November, when, on the third Thursday of the month, that year's vintage of Beaujolais – then barely two months old – is released for immediate consumption. In good vintages this is a charming frivolity to be enjoyed uncritically with friends; in bad vintages it is an acidic public relations stunt that would be better avoided.

The light reds from Beaujolais and the Loire are ideal wines to take on a picnic. They need no particular care and attention, such as decanting, and their soft fruitiness makes them an undemanding pleasure to drink.

Gamay goes well with salads, cold meats, savoury tarts,
and is just right with roast duck, roast veal or chicken.
Perhaps surprisingly, it is also perfect with grilled tuna.

grenache

Grenache is the primary grape of the southern Rhône's Châteauneuf-du-Pape and is one of the ingredients of Spain's finest wine, Vega Sicilia. It is the world's second most planted red variety.

Grenache produces pale wines that are high in alcohol with pleasant hints of sweetness, making the grape ideal for blending with other varieties such as Cinsault, Carignan, Mourvèdre and Syrah. On account of its low tannins and fruity flavour, Grenache is especially successful in producing rosés.

In France, Grenache is grown mainly in Languedoc–Roussillon and the southern Rhône, where it provides up to 80 per cent of the Châteauneuf-du-Pape blend as well as being the dominant variety in the wines of Gigondas and the region's sought-after rosés such as Tavel, Lirac, Côtes du Rhône and Côtes du Ventoux. In Roussillon it helps to make some great sweet wines, known as Vins Doux Naturels, such as Banyuls and Rivesaltes.

Grenache is Spain's most widespread red grape. Known there as Garnacha, it

A top-quality Châteauneuf-du-Pape should be drunk with hefty meat dishes or strong cheeses.

is an important part of the Rioja blend, where it softens the rougher edges of Tempranillo. There are producers in Navarra who like to use Grenache on its own, to make soft, drinkable wines notably high in alcohol.

Plenty of Grenache is grown in Australia, especially in the Barossa Valley, where much of it goes into jug wines, and it is becoming increasingly popular in California, where it is used in Rhône-style blends.

malbec

Malbec ripens early and makes soft wines low in tannin and acidity that are marked by spicy blackberry and violet flavours. It was once an integral part of Bordeaux's blends, but has fallen out of favour recently, often being regarded as no better than a poor man's Merlot.

Although Malbec blends well with Cabernet Sauvignon, nowadays in Bordeaux – where it is known as Cot or Pressac – it is seen as having had its day. In fact the region's only areas which still regard it with any respect are Bourg and Blaye – where the vineyards are more or less divided equally between Malbec, Cabernet Sauvignon and Merlot – and St Émilion.

Elsewhere in France, Malbec manages to cling on in the Loire, where wine makers blend it with other varieties such as Gamay and Cabernet Franc.

The variety is popular in North and South America. Producers in California continue to use Malbec in the old Bordeaux manner, blending it with the traditional varieties of Cabernet Sauvignon, Merlot and Petit Verdot in their Meritage wines. It is grown with some success in Chile, while the wine makers of Argentina, where it is the third most planted variety, are more adventurous, making highly successful single-varietal wines from the grape – probably the only region in the world to do so.

Malbec is going great guns in Argentina and is still favoured in Cahors in south-west France, where – known as Auxerrois – it is part of the region's celebrated 'black wine'.

mourvèdre

Originally from Catalonia, where it is called Monastrell, Mourvèdre is now most associated with the south of France, where it plays its part in making the solid, fruity, everyday drinking wines of the region that are, as yet, rarely exported. In the southern Rhône, Mourvèdre is one of thirteen permitted varieties used in the Grenache-based blend that makes Châteauneuf-du-Pape, adding colour, spice and structure to the wine.

Of the many southern French wines to which Mourvèdre adds its fresh-fruit flavours, the best-known are Bandol (which must comprise at least 50 per cent), Cassis, Corbières, Côtes du Roussillon, Côtes du Rhône–Villages and Palette. In most of these wines, Mourvèdre is blended with Cinsault, Syrah, Carignan or Grenache, and it must be admitted that it struggles to escape from the shadows of such varieties.

As Monastrell, it is Spain's second most important black grape after Garnacha (Grenache). It is well suited to the warm climate, making the big, heavy reds and rosés of Valencia and Alicante.

Also known as Mataro, Mourvèdre can be found in both California, where some interesting single varietal wines are being made, and in Australia. It is also used to make rough local wine in Algeria.

Mourvèdre's wines have a blackberry scent and are peppery and spicy on the palate, but their chewiness and high tannin content mean that they are best when blended with other varieties, and it battles to find an identity of its own.

nebbiolo

Italy's answer to Syrah, Nebbiolo makes the big, dark, tannic wines of Barolo and Barbaresco in the north-west region of Piedmont. Its name derives from the *nebbia*, the fog that creeps over the Piedmontese hills.

Usually regarded as Italy's finest wines, Barolo and Barbaresco both spend regulated periods in oak barrels before their release for sale. Barolo is seen as the more robust and long-lived of these two massive wines, while Barbaresco is considered more elegant and refined; neither of them is cheap.

Other wines made from Nebbiolo include Gattinara, Ghemme and Spanna, the latter wines usually being a blend of other varieties too, which makes them gentler and more approachable than the big two.

The grape's wines are rich, full-bodied, chewy and tannic. Deep in colour, the wines are intense and complex and often identifiable by their aromas of violets, raspberries, prunes and chocolate. They usually require plenty of ageing, although some producers are experimenting with modern-style wines that are softer and more approachable and that require less ageing.

Nebbiolo's wines are invariably high in alcohol, usually 13 per cent or over: they are certainly neither for the faint-hearted nor the aperitif wine drinker.

Although it can produce wines of striking intensity and is recognized as one of the world's finest varieties, Nebbiolo is scarcely grown anywhere other than in north west Italy, although some enterprising wine makers are giving it a go in California.

Barolo and Barbaresco go especially well with game such as venison and hare, and are hard to beat as accompaniments to a winter's Sunday roast.

tempranillo

Tempranillo is to Spain what Cabernet Sauvignon is to France. It puts the grit into the country's most highly regarded red wines, most famously as the major component of Rioja.

Tempranillo is found throughout Spain. Although it is sometimes made into single-varietal wines, it is usually blended with other varieties. In its strongholds of Rioja Alta and Rioja Alavesa, for example, it is blended with Garnacha, Mazuelo, Graciano and Viura. In Ribera del Duero, combined with the varieties that produce claret in Bordeaux, it makes Spain's finest wine – Vega Sicilia. The major red variety in Valdepeñas and La Mancha (where it is known as Cencibel), it is also grown in Costers del Segre, Utiel-Requena, Navarre, Somontano and Penedès.

Tempranillo has good colour and fine ageing potential. With few aromas of its own, it usually smells more of the oak it is aged in, although it can give off the odd whiff of strawberries, leather, tobacco, toffee and spice.

Tempranillo is most closely associated with Spain, but it can also be found in the Midi in France, in Portugal - where, known as Tinta Roriz, it is one of the many varieties used in the production of port - and in South America, especially in the Mendoza region of Argentina.

Tempranillo in the form of Rioja goes especially well with rich meat dishes such as casseroles, roast duck, goose and lamb, as well as with more simple fare, such as spaghetti bolognese and lasagne.

Sangiovese is the major grape behind such celebrated Italian wines as Chianti, Brunello di Montalcino and Vino Nobile di Montepulciano.

sangiovese

Along with Nebbiolo, Sangiovese is seen as one of Italy's top red grapes; it is the most widely planted red grape in the country, with its stronghold in central and southern regions. Despite the grape's high reputation, the quality of its wines varies dramatically, largely because so many different clones of the variety exist.

Whatever its perceived shortcomings elsewhere might be, Sangiovese does, unquestionably, make the finest red wines of Tuscany. Chianti is made there, with Sangiovese providing up to 90 per cent of the blend. Chianti Classico is the highest quality Chianti, and at its best should taste of fresh herbs and cherries.

Sangiovese also provides up to 80 per cent of the Vino Nobile di Montepulciano blend, while under its pseudonym, Brunello, it is left unblended, making what is in effect a single-varietal wine – Brunello di Montalcino, a big, dark wine with plenty of tannin.

As well as its role in traditional Tuscan wines, Sangiovese is also an important component (along with Cabernet Sauvignon and Merlot) in making the more modern wines known as the 'Super Tuscans'. Owing to the fact that non-indigenous grapes are used, such wines remained unclassified for many years, until the authorities could ignore them no longer. They now enjoy their own classification, with prices to match.

Sangiovese doesn't stray much outside Italy, although there are some plantings of the variety in Mendoza province in Argentina and in California.

Chianti is a good partner for most simple chicken dishes and, inevitably, goes perfectly with pastas and pizzas.

cinsault

Grown mainly in Languedoc-Roussillon, Cinsault is highly productive, making wines that are high in acidity and low in tannin. France's fourth most planted variety, Cinsault is used chiefly in blends to provide spice, perfume, smoothness and fruit, though some single-varietal rosés are made too.

In Languedoc-Roussillon (notably in Hérault, Gard and Aude) it is usually blended with Carignan or Grenache. In the southern Rhône, where it makes deeper-coloured, more concentrated wines, it is frequently blended with Mourvèdre, Grenache or Syrah. One of the thirteen approved grape varieties used in making Châteauneuf-du-Pape,

Cinsault is also an obligatory ingredient in the basic Côtes du Rhône-Villages.

Its high productivity led Cinsault to be widely planted in South Africa, where, for some reason, it is sometimes known as Hermitage. South Africa's own variety, called Pinotage, is a cross between Cinsault and Pinot Noir.

The grape blends especially well with Cabernet Sauvignon and Syrah, a combination that has proved particularly successful in southern France, Australia and Lebanon where, most famously, it is used at Château Musar.

petit verdot

Petit Verdot makes full-bodied wines noted for their depth of colour and spicy, peppery characteristics.

Petit Verdot is a high-quality grape that is not dissimilar to Syrah in its deep colour and peppery spiciness. It is little seen outside Bordeaux, where it has long been used as a sort of vinous monosodium glutamate, adding a touch of zip to claret's triumvirate of Cabernet Sauvignon, Merlot and Cabernet Franc by enhancing the blend's colour, flavour and tannin.

When used in such a way it usually comprises as little as 2-3 per cent of the blend and certainly never more than 10 per cent. It is used chiefly in the southern Médoc, where the soil produces light wines that are more in need of an extra dash of flavour than the wines of the northern Médoc.

The grape is used in a similar manner in countries such as California and Chile, adding oomph to blended wines.

pinotage

Pinotage is South African through and through, having been developed there in 1925 as a cross between Pinot Noir and Cinsault. Even the name Pinotage is a hybrid, being a cross between Pinot Noir and Hermitage, the South African name for Cinsault. Although the main home of Pinotage is South Africa, there are also plantings in California and scatterings elsewhere.

Pinotage wines are invariably deep purple in colour and are often characterized on the nose by remarkably unenticing whiffs of burnt rubber.

When on form, Pinotage can make wines of fruit and freshness, marked by raspberry-like flavours, but all too frequently it is one-dimensional and flat. Frequently tannic and chewy, Pinotage is sometimes compared to Syrah, although it lacks much of that grape's style and panache. Styles vary between fruity wines designed to be drunk young and full-bodied wines that need ageing; in either event, despite its qualities and its individuality, Pinotage remains an acquired taste.

Drink Pinotage with casseroles and roast meats, and richly sauced dishes.

zinfandel

Zinfandel is known as California's own grape, being the region's only indigenous variety and its most widely planted. It is believed to be related to the little-known Primitivo grape found in Italy.

California remains Zinfandel's favoured home, but it is grown with increasing success in Australia, South America and South Africa. Zinfandel produces wines similar to those of Cabernet Sauvignon, albeit with higher levels of alcohol and softer tannins, which may be drunk young or allowed to develop with age.

The range of wines produced by Zinfandel is bewildering: as well as top-quality, full-bodied red wine, it makes semi-sweet white wine, 'blush' wine, jug wine, sparkling wine and even fortified wine. Most commercially successful are the so-called 'white Zinfandels' (which are usually pink), blended wines that may include other grapes too, such as the white variety Muscat. The resulting semi-sweet wines are the closest that anyone has come to creating alcoholic candyfloss in liquid form, and are best avoided.

Drink the big red Zinfandels with barbecued foods, chili con carne or roast lamb.

red wine:
vintages

Differences between one wine and another depend on the grapes, the soil in which the grapes are grown, the way in which the wines are made, and the weather. In New World wine regions such as California and Australia, blessed with constant temperatures and clement weather, variations between years are less pronounced than in Europe. There, although poor vintages are getting rarer owing to improved wine technology, a late frost, hail storms or lack of sunshine can mean the difference between success and failure for a vintage.

A blend of two or more vintages will be described as non-vintage or NV, and will show no date on the label, as is often the case with cheap wines. The listing of a vintage date on a label must not be taken as a guarantee of the quality of that wine – except with fine wines – but rather as simply a matter of record and a note of the wine's age. Top red wines can take from 5 to 25 years to mature, although there is a growing trend among wine makers to produce wine for relatively early drinking.

Recent fine vintages for claret include 1982, 1985, 1986, 1988, 1989, 1990, 1995, 1996, 1998, 2000, 2001, 2003, 2005, 2006, 2009, 2010.

Recent fine vintages for red burgundy include 1985, 1988, 1989, 1990, 1993, 1995, 1996, 1999, 2002, 2005, 2009, 2010.

ageing

Most top-quality red wines are aged in oak barrels prior to bottling, allowing them to mature and to reach their full potential. They become less tannic, smoother and more complex, as they age, characteristics that are further enhanced by subsequent maturation in bottle.

No wood is as good for ageing wine as oak, with great differences being achieved according to the size of the barrel, the type of oak used (usually *Limousin*, *Allier* or *Tronçais* from France) and by whether it is old oak or new oak, or a combination of the two. New oak contains vanillin, which gives wines that have been in barrel for any length of time a noticeable aroma of vanilla.

Some producers prefer not to use oak because they feel that it imparts too much flavour to their wines, and so they use stainless steel instead. Other producers feel that oak is essential, while some even use oak chips as a quicker, but less satisfactory, method of imparting the unique flavour associated with oak.

red wine: quality classifications

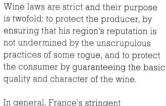

Wine laws are strict and their purpose is twofold: to protect the producer, by ensuring that his region's reputation is not undermined by the unscrupulous practices of some rogue, and to protect the consumer by guaranteeing the basic quality and character of the wine.

In general, France's stringent *Appellation d'Origine Contrôlée* (AOC) laws give a guarantee of a wine's origins and authenticity of a grape variety, but without guaranteeing quality. The categories below AOC are *Vin Délimité de Qualité Supérieure* (VDQS), *Vin de Pays* and *Vin de Table*: these are for lower-quality wines and have less rigid restrictions applied to their production.

Italy has a similar system, the *Denominazione di Origine Controllata* (DOC), but many top producers consider it too restrictive and make great wines that have to be classified as *Vino da Tavola*. A new classification, *Indicazione Geografica Tipica* (IGT) has been added to alleviate some of the confusion.

In Bordeaux the top 60 wines in the Médoc are classified as *Grands Crus Classés* or Classified Growths, and these represent the aristocracy of the thousands of Bordeaux châteaux in five divisions. One step lower come the *Crus Bourgeois* or Bourgeois Growths, still excellent wines and usually good value. In Burgundy, a classification of *Premiers Crus* and *Grands Crus* identify the best vineyards, again based on location.

Spain and Italy designate their wines *Reserva* or *Riserva* to indicate a certain period in oak, a treatment usually kept for the best wines, unlike France, whose categories relate to location.

In 1983 the USA set up the American Viticultural Area (AVA) system to emulate France's AOC laws but, as in the rest of the New World, American wines remain free from the rigid restrictions that govern European wines – something that is often more than made up for by producers' giving extraordinarily detailed information on back labels.

Virtually every European wine-growing region
has its own rules about which grapes may be used,
where and by what method they might be grown and vinified:
where they do not exist, individual producers
will often create a structure of their own.

red wine: storing & serving

It pays to look after your wine properly, be it half a dozen bottles of inexpensive wine from the supermarket or a case of claret that needs time to mature. Don't worry if you haven't got a cellar; a bottle of wine is like a baby - far sturdier than you might imagine. As long as you store bottles with corks on their sides (to ensure that the corks don't dry out), and avoid exposing them to long periods of fluctuating temperatures, damp, strong aromas, bright lights and vibrations, you can be certain that the wine will stay in good condition.

Increasingly, bottles are sealed with screwtaps. If stoppered with a cork, remove the capsule from the top of the bottle with a foil-cutter or a strong thumbnail. Use a decent corkscrew to remove the cork - the Screwpull is best.

Mature red wines and vintage ports are liable to leave a sediment and need decanting, a process that also helps the wines to 'breathe' and release their flavours. (A plastic funnel, coffee filter-paper and a clean empty bottle are just as effective for decanting as anything grander.)

Red wines are best served at room temperature, although lighter ones such as those from the Loire and Beaujolais can be delicious chilled. When in company, taste the wine first to check that it is all right before filling your guess classes. Fill no more than a quarter of your glass and look at the wine. It should be clear and bright without any cloudiness or haziness. Holding the stem, swirl the glass around to release the bouquet. Put your nose to the glass and inhale deeply; the wine should smell clean and fresh. Almost anything that might be wrong with a wine can be detected on the nose, by odours of mustiness perhaps, or dampness. Take a mouthful of the wine, drawing air into the mouth as you do so. Roll the liquid around your tongue and then spit or swallow. What is it like? Is it sweet or dry, light or full-bodied? Does it remind you of anything? The taste of a fine wine remains in the mouth, and its many components - its acidity, alcohol, fruit and tannin - should have combined so pleasantly that you want nothing more than to take another sip.

white wine

bottle shapes & sizes

In this age of designer chic, European wine producers are less strict than they were about using the traditional bottles of their respective regions; while producers from the New World are divided between those who use the shapes most associated with each particular variety and those who bottle their wines in whatever shape pleases them. Nevertheless, the shape and colour of a wine bottle remain useful tools for identifying the style and type of wine inside.

As a rule, the sweet and dry white wines of Bordeaux come in high-shouldered bottles of green or clear glass while New World Sauvignons come in any manner of bottle. White burgundies, Chablis, white Rhônes and many New World Chardonnays are in green or clear bottles with sloping shoulders; while the aromatic wines of Alsace, Germany and beyond come in tall, slender bottles. Those from Alsace are green, whereas German wines have a further distinction, in that wines from the Mosel (known as Moselles) come in green bottles and those from the Rhine (known as Hocks) come in brown bottles.

Apart from rare exceptions, champagne and sparkling wines come in dark green bottles with sloping shoulders and a pronounced indentation in the base called a punt. Champagne producers are famous for using outsized bottles for their wines, without which no grand celebration is complete. Sizes range from a quarter-bottle to a Nebuchadnezzar.

Quarter-bottle = 18.75cl
Half-bottle = 37.5cl
Bottle = 75cl
Magnum = 2 bottles
Double magnum = 4 bottles
Jeroboam = 4 bottles
Rehoboam = 6 bottles
Methuselah = 8 bottles
Salmanazar = 12 bottles
Balthazar = 16 bottles
Nebuchadnezzar = 20 bottles

white wine:
labels explained

Among the items of information that must, by law, appear on a label on the front or back of a bottle are:

- the wine's name
- the size of the bottle
- the vintage (if there is one)
- the wine's alcoholic strength
- the producer's name and address
- the name of the bottler (if different from the producer)
- the name of the importer
- the name of the shipper (if different from the importer)
- the wine's quality level
- whether the wine contains sulphites
- where the wine was bottled
- the wine's country of origin
- the wine's region and appellation (if relevant)

Some labels also include the grape variety.

Wine labels are there to inform, and if read correctly will tell you all you need to know about the wine itself. Most countries now insist on displaying a government health warning about the hazards of drinking wine (with not a word about the proven benefits). Wines sold in the USA, for example, must show stern admonitions about the perils of alcohol from the Surgeon General, while those sold in France caution pregant women not to drink.

The white wines with the most perplexing labels are those from Germany, and not only because they are often written in indecipherable Gothic script. Information on these labels includes the following terms for the six categories of ripeness.

Kabinett = the driest level of quality wine.

Spätlese = wines made from late-picked grapes.

Auslese = wines made from selected bunches of very ripe grapes.

Trockenbeerenauslese = wines made from dried grapes or those attacked by 'noble rot'.

Beerenauslese = wines made from individually selected grapes.

Eiswein = wines made from grapes picked when frozen, which concentrates the sugar in the juice.

These terms can be linked to levels of sweetness, from Kabinett, the most dry, to the incredibly honeyed Trockenbeerenauslese and intensely sweet Eiswein.

Wine labels are there to help you, and if read correctly
will tell you everything you need to know about the wine itself.

white wine: single varietals & blends

A single varietal is a wine made wholly, or almost wholly, from a single type of grape – Chardonnay, perhaps, Sauvignon Blanc or Sylvaner. Rules about varietals differ from region to region. For example, in Australia 80 per cent of the wine must come from the named variety, while in the USA it is 75 per cent.

In Europe the tradition is to name the wines after the place of origin rather than after the variety, Alsace being a notable exception. Therefore, if you know you like single-varietal Chardonnays from California or Australia, say, it is helpful to know that all white burgundies, such as Pouilly-Fuissé, Puligny-Montrachet or Meursault, are also single varietals, being 100 per cent Chardonnay.

The art of blending is to marry the wines of two or more varieties together to make a wine greater than the sum of its parts. The process can also encompass different vintages, as in the case of non-vintage champagnes or standard 'house white' burgundies that are blended in such a way as to ensure that they always taste the same.

The blending of different varieties occurs less often in white wines than it does in red wines. In France, for example, the great wines of Sancerre and Pouilly Fumé, are 100 per cent Sauvignon Blanc, while white burgundies and Chablis are 100 per cent Chardonnay. Champagne is usually a blend of three varieties, but producers do also make champagnes from both Chardonnay and Pinot Noir on their own.

Some blends are seen only in the New World; in Australia, Semillon/Chardonnay blends are common, but this is an example of a combination that would be prohibited by the restrictive wine laws in most areas of France.

There are strong arguments in favour of blends and of single varietals – arguments that are revisited whenever two or more winemakers are gathered together. Neither style is better than the other. They are simply different, and just because you like the subtlety of one particular blend it does not mean that you won't also appreciate the purity of a particular single varietal.

The art of blending is to marry the wines of two or more varieties together to make a wine greater than the sum of its parts.

chardonnay

Chardonnay is without doubt the world's most popular grape variety. Purists might argue that Riesling makes the finer and more elegant wine, but that view is not reflected in public opinion. Chardonnay is easy to grow, has good acid levels, high alcohol, ages well, blends well with other varieties – and winemakers and wine drinkers can't get enough of it. Since it is difficult to make a poor wine from the grape, it is rare to find a bad Chardonnay.

Chardonnay is responsible for champagne and Chablis, and for such well-known white burgundies as Puligny-Montrachet, Meursault, Corton-Charlemagne and Pouilly-Fuissé. It varies in taste according to where it is grown, on account of variations in climate and wine-makers' techniques. Chardonnays from Burgundy tend to be elegant and refined compared to the big-boned wines from Australia or California, where warmer

Forget the red wine for once and drink a fine oak-aged
Chardonnay from Burgundy or Australia with a hearty meat
casserole or roast veal, or a Chablis with cheeses such
as Brie and Camembert.

climates result in riper grapes and more oak is
used. But even in two neighbouring areas there
can be pronounced differences, for while white
burgundies can be nutty or toasty, the wines of
Chablis can be steely and flinty.

Chardonnay does spectacularly well in Australia,
New Zealand, South Africa, South America, Italy
and Spain. It is especially loved by Californians,
in whose state it is the most planted grape variety.
In fact, to many Americans, the word Chardonnay
is synonymous with white wine, so ubiquitous is
the variety. But despite these major successes
elsewhere, Burgundy remains its spiritual home.

One cannot speak of Chardonnay without also
referring to oak, with which it has a special
relationship. Oak barrels draw out Chardonnay's
best characteristics and give the wine aromas
of vanilla, toast and nuts. Oaked and unoaked
Chardonnays can be very different; try both.

There are many different types of Riesling with different names which can be confusing. In California the true Riesling is called Johannisberg Riesling; in Australia it is known as Rhine Riesling; and in South Africa as Weisser Riesling.

riesling

True Riesling is the most elegant of grapes and is most at home in Germany, where all the top wines, be they sweet or dry, are Rieslings. The sweet wines are usually affected by noble rot and range in sweetness through Auslese and Beerenauslese to Trockenbeerenauslese.

German Rieslings are frequently light in alcohol and age remarkably well, gaining rich honey flavours as they do so. The grape should be instantly identifiable in the glass, marked out by its distinctive aromas of petrol, peaches, melons, apples and limes.

Remarkably - considering that it is regarded as one of the world's finest grapes, if not the finest - you won't find Riesling in France, other than in Alsace where it is considered top dog and makes fresh, lively wines, which, while delicate, are fuller and higher in alcohol than those from neighbouring Germany.

The grape is also widely grown in Austria, making dry, concentrated wines, and in Italy's Friuli and Alto Adige, where it makes light, elegant and aromatic wines.

Riesling is grown in Marlborough, New Zealand, producing wines of excellent acidity and delicacy, and it also features in South Africa and Chile. Most of California is too warm to produce dry Riesling - the drinking public seems only to want Chardonnay anyway - but both Washington state and Ontario in Canada exploit the grape's preference for cool conditions to make wines of real delicacy. Superb examples can be found in Australia in the Barossa, Eden and Clare Valleys.

Drier German Rieslings go well with Pacific Rim cooking and other spicy food, while the sweet ones are perfect with fruit, nuts or desserts.

sauvignon blanc

Sauvignon Blanc is one of the world's major grape varieties, celebrated as much for its distinctive, steely-dry single varietals as it is for its role in the world's finest dessert wines.

France's most celebrated Sauvignon Blancs are Sancerre and Pouilly Fumé from the Loire, where producers don't believe in blending the variety, which is sometimes called Blanc Fumé. They prefer to make single varietals that are fermented and aged in stainless-steel vats rather than in oak, creating wines that are crisp and clean-flavoured with a smoky, mineral quality. Other, lesser-known but good-value Loire wines made from Sauvignon Blanc include Ménétou-Salon, Quincy, Reuilly and Sauvignon de Touraine.

Sauvignon Blanc is more acidic than Chardonnay; to some, this crispness is preferable to the soft butteriness of Chardonnay. The grape is notable for its aromas of freshly cut grass, blackcurrant leaves, gooseberries, asparagus and – remarkably, but undeniably – cat's pee. Some people would argue that, impressive as

Sauvignon Blanc is on its own, it is only when combined with Sémillon that it achieves true greatness. In Bordeaux the dry wines of Entre-Deux-Mers and Graves are blends of Sauvignon Blanc and Sémillon (usually aged in oak), as are the great dessert wines of Barsac and Sauternes and the lesser ones of Ste-Croix du Mont and Monbazillac.

New Zealand produces some stunning Sauvignon Blancs, giving the wines of the Loire a close run for their money. In California, too, Sauvignon Blanc flourishes, thanks to Robert Mondavi, who pioneered the variety in North America, originally calling it Fumé Blanc. Now second in popularity to Chardonnay in the USA, Sauvignon Blanc produces wines that tend to be less tropical than those of New Zealand and less lean than those of the Loire. The grape is also a huge success in Chile and South Africa.

Apart from the sweet wines and fuller dry wines of Bordeaux, most Sauvignon Blancs are best drunk while they are still young – that is, within three or four years of the vintage.

Being light, crisp and refreshing, Sauvignon Blancs make excellent aperitifs as well as enhancing most poultry and fish dishes.

Single-varietal Sémillon goes well with smoked fish, such as trout, haddock or mackerel.

sémillon

Sémillon makes deep-yellow wines that are full-bodied, high in both alcohol and aroma, low in acid, and which age extremely well, being particularly well suited to oak. Sémillon is one of the great unsung grapes of the world, and many people consume it without having heard of it, most notably in the wines of Bordeaux, where Sémillon adds structure to the dry wines of the Graves and the sweet ones of Sauternes and Barsac. It has become more prominent recently thanks to its role in blended wines from the New World, most of which are labelled varietally.

Unblended, Sémillon is apt to make undistinguished, forgettable wines, but when it is combined with Sauvignon Blanc, great things happen. Sauvignon Blanc provides the acidity and aromas, while Sémillon softens Sauvignon Blanc's rougher edges to make sublime wines that are often greater than either variety can make on its own.

Sémillon is susceptible to noble rot and provides the lion's share of the blends that go to make up the finest Sauternes and Barsacs, whose rich, intensely honeyed and utterly delicious wines usually include about 80 per cent Sémillon, 20 per cent Sauvignon Blanc and a slurp of Muscadelle.

Australia (where Semillon has a non-accented 'e') makes some fine single varietals, most famously in the Hunter Valley where it's something of a star, perhaps proving to the doubters that the grape can stand alone. It is also blended very successfully with Chardonnay and makes fine dessert wines. Single-varietal Sémillons are also made in South Africa, mainly in Paarl, Wellington and Franschhoek Valleys, and in Chile, where it once provided two-thirds of all white wine produced, much of it pretty basic – the grape tending to be fat and oily – and little of which was exported.

Chenin Blanc is an extraordinary grape in that it can produce still and sparkling wine, sweet and dry wine, fortified wine and spirits.

chenin blanc

The Chenin Blanc grape comes originally from the Loire Valley in France, where it is often known as Pineau de la Loire, and where its versatility is much in evidence. It is there that it produces such wines as the dry Savennières from Anjou, the dry, the sparkling or the utterly delicious sweet Vouvrays from Touraine, the late-harvest Côteaux du Layons and the sparkling wines of Saumur.

Thousands of litres of indifferent and sharp table wine are made from Chenin Blanc in the Loire too, indicating that it is not at its best when made into a dry wine.

Its susceptibility to botrytis, the noble rot that concentrates the sugar in the grape, makes Chenin Blanc ideal for producing dessert wines, the best of which can last for decades, gaining beautiful golden hues and rich honey flavours as they age. Its high natural acidity is perfect for making sparkling wine and it is an important component in the blend responsible for the world's oldest sparkling wine, Blanquette de Limoux from the Midi.

Chenin Blanc seems to do best in marginal climates and it is grown successfully in New Zealand and in South Africa, where, once known as Steen, it is the country's most popular variety, making increasingly delicious wines.

Elsewhere in the New World, Chenin Blanc is rarely accorded the respect that it receives in the Loire or South Africa. In Australia it is used mainly for blending into commercial wines, while in California the clamour for Chardonnay and Sauvignon Blanc means that there is currently little consumer interest in it.

Nothing goes better with strawberries and cream
or a fruit tart than a sweet Vouvray.

Gewurztraminer goes well with strong cheeses and spicy food such as Thai or Chinese cuisine, as well as with smoked salmon and Pacific Rim cooking.

Gewurztraminer may be the most difficult variety to spell and to pronounce (it is now generally spelt without an umlaut), but its deep golden colour and exotic and heady aromas of lychees, spice, flowers, peaches and apricots are unforgettable, making it a cinch to spot at blind tastings.

Although it is grown throughout Europe and is supposed to have originated in Italy's Alto Adige (where it is still known as Traminer Aromatico), Gewurztraminer is most at home in Alsace. Here the variety is at its most pungent, making sweet-smelling but intensely dry wines, high in alcohol, low in acidity and bursting with spicy flavours. In great years, rich and honeyed late-harvest wines, known as *vendanges tardives*, are made, as too, in exceptional years, are botrytis-affected wines known as *séléction de grains nobles*.

Gewürz is the German word for spice, and Gewurztraminer is highly regarded both in Germany, especially in Rheinpfalz just over the border from Alsace, and in Austria. The grape does best in cool climates, and in the New World it is happiest in New Zealand, although there are some plantings in Australia too. In California it is grown only in the cooler areas such as Los Carneros, Anderson Valley and Monterey County, where it makes scented wines, noticeably softer and less spicy than those of Alsace. Some wines are also being made successfully in Oregon in America's Pacific north-west.

gewurztraminer

marsanne

Marsanne is a vigorous grape that produces deep-coloured, brown-tinged wine high in alcohol with a distinctive and heady aroma reminiscent of apples, pears, glue, nuts, spice and almonds.

The grape's full flavour, coupled with a low acidity, means that it is ideal for blending; the variety with which it is inextricably linked being Roussanne. It is a highly successful partnership, responsible for such white wines of the northern Rhône as Côtes du Rhône Blanc, Crozes-Hermitage, Hermitage and St-Joseph. Marsanne is also one of the grapes permitted in the blend that makes the southern Rhône's comparatively rare white Châteauneuf-du-Pape.

Although Marsanne is traditionally seen as making long-lived, full-bodied wines that can sometimes be dull when young, modern winemaking techniques are changing such perceptions, and fruity, perfumed wines are being produced for early consumption. When

A fine white Rhône is perfect with heavily sauced lobster or crab or with fish dishes such as grilled tuna or turbot.

young, its wines are flowery and aromatic; when old, they are rich and nutty; indeed, it seems nowadays that only in its middle age is it dull. Increasingly grown in the Midi, Marsanne makes fleshy white wines in Cassis, and the dry, sweet, still and sparkling wines of St-Péray, south of Cornas in the northern Rhône. It is a permitted ingredient in the northern Rhône's Syrah-dominated red Hermitage, and is grown successfully in the Valais, in Switzerland, where it is known as Ermitage Blanc.

As for the New World, Marsanne has been grown in Victoria in Australia since the 1860s, making big, long-lived wines, but it is seen only occasionally in California, where it appears as either single varietals or blended with its old Rhône friend Roussanne.

pinot blanc

Found in almost every wine region in the world,
Pinot Blanc is best known in Alsace (where, unusually
for a French wine region, it is sold under its varietal name)
and in Italy, where it is an important part of
the blend that makes Soave.

Pinot Blanc is not dissimilar to Chardonnay, to which it was once
thought to be related, although it is not nearly so flavoursome,
complex or sophisticated. At its best it should be fresh, lively
and appealing with flavours of yeast and apples backed up by
the faintest hints of honey. But although it is invariably light and
pleasing on the palate, it never really seems to have a great deal to
say. Its high acidity makes it ideal for making sparkling wines and
it is used as the base for most of Alsace's fizzy Crémant d'Alsace.

In Alsace, Pinot Blanc also makes drinkable, if undramatic, dry
white wines, the lightest of the region which, while well regarded,
are usually eclipsed by those of Pinot Gris. Modest amounts are
also grown in Burgundy, usually for blending with Chardonnay
into the region's basic white wine - Bourgogne Blanc. It is grown all
over Italy - where it is called Pinot Bianco - notably in the Veneto,
Alto Adige and Lombardy, where it makes pleasant sparkling wine.

Alsace Pinot Blanc goes especially well with fish pâtés,
light salads and pasta with seafood sauces.

As Weissburgunder, Pinot Blanc is increasingly popular in Germany, making both dry and sweet wines - especially in Baden and Rheinpfalz - and it is grown throughout Austria, even being used to make botrytized Trockenbeerenauslese.

Pinot Blanc is ignored by much of the New World. Some is grown in Chile, and a few producers grow it successfully in California; confusingly, much of what is called Pinot Blanc in California is in fact Melon de Bourgogne.

Pinot Gris is low in acid and goes especially well with food; those from
Alsace in particular are marvellous with that region's choucroute
and cheeses, as well as with cold meats and hot or cold lobster.

pinot gris (grigio)

Pinot Gris produces fragrant white wines of depth and substance, with styles ranging from crisp, light and dry, to rich, full and honeyed. At its best, it makes a fine alternative to white burgundy and can be full-bodied enough to drink with dishes that are more usually accompanied by red wines. Although technically a white grape, Pinot Gris is a mutation of the red Pinot Noir and it can produce wines that are almost rosé in colour.

Pinot Gris thrives in Alsace (where it is sometimes still known as Tokay d'Alsace or Tokay Pinot-Gris), producing not only big, smoky, dry wines but also the remarkably intense *vendanges tardives*. Around Touraine, in the Loire, it makes charming rosés, and in Valais in Switzerland it results in rich, full wines. While Pinot Gris is oily and fat in Alsace, it is lighter, spritzier and more acidic in Italy, where - known as Pinot Grigio - it is grown mainly in Friuli, Lombardy and in small areas of Emilia-Romagna.

Germany grows more Pinot Gris (known there as Rulander) than any other country, making juicy wines of low acidity and spicy aroma, especially in Baden, Württemberg and Rheinpfalz.

It is catching on in the New World, growing in popularity in New Zealand California, especially among those bored by the ubiquity of Chardonnay, and there are some plantings of Pinot Gris in Mexico and Willamette Valley in Oregon.

roussanne

Roussanne is the more refined half of the vinous double act it performs with Marsanne. In the northern Rhône, in particular, the two grapes are inextricably linked, joining forces to produce the white versions of Hermitage, Crozes-Hermitage and St-Joseph, as well as being permitted in small quantities in the red Hermitage blend, adding softness to the otherwise unblended Syrah.

Roussanne is less widely grown than Marsanne, not least because it is prone to powdery mildew and rot and has an irregular yield, but it is the more stylish and polished of the two, and its wines age more gracefully. In the southern Rhône it is used in the blends that make both the red and the white Châteauneuf-du-Pape.

Roussanne is also grown in Languedoc-Roussillon, where the warm climate ensures that its tendency to ripen late is less of a problem than it is in the northern Rhône, or in Savoie in eastern France, where small amounts of single-varietal Roussanne can be found if you look hard enough.

Roussanne has a spicier flavour than Marsanne, and while its wines are delicious when young, with a tendency to blossom in later years, they can, like those of Marsanne, be a bit grumpy in middle age. The two grapes also combine to make the Rhône's *méthode traditionelle* wine, St-Péray, a full-flavoured sparkler with an almost nutty taste.

White Rhônes go well with smoked eel, smoked salmon and gravadlax.

Viognier has now become extremely fashionable among growers and drinkers alike, having gained its reputation by producing the extraordinarily intense dry white wines from the tiny vineyards of Château Grillet and Condrieu next door to Côte Rôtie in the northern Rhône. Restaurants that had never heard of Viognier 20 years ago are now stocking several examples of the variety, which are well worth seeking out, although they are likely to be expensive.

Good Viogniers are big-boned beauties with alluring, but fleeting, scents of peaches and apricots, comparable in their headiness of aroma and pungency of flavour to Gewurztraminer. The less good examples can be overpowering and lacking in finesse.

Viognier is something of a curiosity in that it has long been used as an aromatic addition to the great red wines of Côte Rôtie, being vinified alongside the red grape Syrah and often comprising up to 20 per cent of the final blend.

Viognier is being seen more often in Italy, New Zealand, Chile and Australia as well as in other parts of France, such as Languedoc–Roussillon, where some notable single varietals are being made and marketed under the name of the variety rather than the geographic location. It has also gained popularity in California.

viognier

The grape has become hugely popular, with producers having to question whether or not investing in a potential money-spinner is worth the drawbacks of the grape's low productivity and its susceptibility to disease.

grüner veltliner

Grüner Veltliner has become very fashionable recently. It is particularly valued as a very successful food wine, combining the lusciousness of Pinot Gris, the bouquet of Riesling and the acidity of Sauvignon Blanc. It is being planted increasingly widely as its reputation spreads, in California, for example, Argentina and even China, although its heartland remains firmly in Austria, where it accounts for around 50% of the vineyard area (compared to barely 2% a couple of generations ago). The finest examples of all come from around the town of Krems, in Lower Austria, where it is capable of exhibiting a wonderful minerality and spicy acidity. But, given that Austria's entire wine production is barely half that of Bordeaux, they are going to have to continue to increase production if Grüner Veltliner is to become the next Viognier.

French country wines made from Colombard are ideal for knocking back, well chilled, at picnics or outdoors on late summer evenings.

Colombard originated in the Charente region of France and used to be distilled to make Cognac and Armagnac. It has been largely supplanted in this role by Ugni Blanc, as Trebbiano is known there, and so growers have turned to making it into simple, undemanding wines such as Vin de Pays des Côtes de Gascogne – crisp and spicy off-dry wines of high acidity and flowery perfume.

Remarkably, this productive but little-known grape is now one of the most widely planted varieties in California where – called French Colombard – it is prized for its ability to make simple crisp wines in a warm climate. For similar reasons it is also widely grown in both Australia and South Africa, where it is often blended with Chenin Blanc to make everyday drinking wines or sparklers.

colombard

müller-thurgau

Müller-Thurgau is a hybrid variety created in 1882 by Dr Hermann Müller, from the Swiss canton of Thurgau, who, in crossing Riesling with Sylvaner, hoped to combine the quality of the former with the early-ripening capability of the latter. At its best, its wines are light, fresh, fruity and fragrant; at worst, they are bland, characterless and lacking in flavour.

Although it's a grape on the wane, it remains widely planted in Germany, making the infamous bottled bubble-gum, Liebfraumilch. The grape ripens almost anywhere, producing huge amounts of extremely dull, medium-dry, and some sweet, wine. The grape has a tendency to be a bit mousy in Germany though, and makes cleaner and fresher wines in Italy's Alto Adige, Luxembourg and in England, where it was once popular.

The grape was once the mainstay of New Zealand's wine industry, producers believing it to be the variety best suited to their climate. It probably makes better wine there than it does anywhere else, but, as the industry has grown and tastes have become more sophisticated, so Chardonnay and Sauvignon Blanc have consigned Müller-Thurgau to kiwi oblivion.

Müller-Thurgau should be drunk on its own or with light, delicately flavoured dishes.

muscat

Muscat is thought to be the oldest variety known to man, its hundreds of different incarnations producing many styles of wine. It may sound odd, but Muscat is the only grape to produce wine that actually tastes and smells of grapes.

One of the grape's best-known strains, Muscat Blanc à Petits Grains, is responsible for the fortified Muscat de Beaumes-de-Venise from the southern Rhône, and, blended with Clairette, the sparkling Clairette de Die in the northern Rhône.

In Greece, Muscat makes the dessert wines of Samos, Pátras and Cephalonia. In Italy, it is the flavour behind Asti Spumante. In Australia, known as Brown Muscat or Frontignan, it makes delicious fortified liqueur wines, as it does in California, where it is known as Muscat Blanc, Muscat Canelli or Muscat Frontignan.

Muscat Ottonel is grown in Alsace for heady dry wines and in Austria for sublime dessert wines. Muscat of Alexandria is usually used for table grapes, but in Spain it is used to make the heavy, sweet fortified wine Moscatel de Málaga and, in Portugal, Moscatel de Setúbal. Orange Muscat and Muscat Hamburg are grown in Australia and California for dessert wine; the latter, known as Black Muscat, is only rarely used.

sylvaner

Sylvaner originated in Austria, where it still thrives, albeit less ubiquitously than it once did. Despite being edged out by its own ungrateful offspring – Müller-Thurgau – as the country's most planted variety, Sylvaner is still much grown in Germany, mainly in Franken, Rheinhessen and Rheinpfalz. In Franken, where Riesling is difficult to ripen, it does especially well.

In France, Sylvaner is virtually unknown outside Alsace, where it makes easy-drinking, rather nondescript wines at the lower end of the price range. Even there, it is planted much less frequently than before. Switzerland remains true to the variety, especially in Valais where it is known as Johannisberg, making quaffable, refreshing wines of no great character. It used to be grown fairly widely in California, but in the charge to plant Sauvignon Blanc and Chardonnay it has all but been forgotten.

Sylvaner from Alsace goes well with onion tarts and quiches and is delicious with bouillabaisse.

A fritto misto eaten on the quayside of an
Italian fishing village, washed downwith
an Orvieto or Frascati, is hard to beat.

trebbiano

No grape produces more of the world's
wine than Trebbiano, and it remains
the most widely planted white variety
in France, where it is known as Ugni
Blanc. The grape is notorious for
producing bland, nondescript wines of
little character, and so, on the principle
that the worse the base wine the better
the brandy, much of it is used for
distillation.

In Italy it appears blended with other
grape varieties in Frascati, Orvieto,
Verdicchio, Soave and Vernaccia di
San Gimignano and was once even
permitted in (red) Chianti Classico.

Trebbiano is also grown in California –
mainly in the San Joaquin Valley – and
in Mexico, in both cases chiefly being
used for distillation.

white wine: vintages

Differences between wines are caused by the grapes, the soil in which they were grown, the way in which the wines were made and, above all, by the weather. In the wine-producing parts of California and Australia, blessed with relatively constant temperatures and clement weather, variations between years are less pronounced than they are in Europe, where a late frost, a hail storm or lack of sunshine can mean the difference between success and failure for a harvest.

If a blend of two or more vintages is used, the resultant wine will be known as non-vintage or NV, and will show no date on the label.

Except in the case of fine wines, the listing of a vintage date on a bottle of wine should not be taken as a guarantee of quality but rather as simply a matter of record and a note of the wine's age.

Recent fine vintages for white burgundy include 1995, 1996, 1997, 2000, 2001, 2002, 2005, 2006, 2009, 2010.

Among recent fine vintages for Sauternes are 1988, 1989, 1990, 1996, 1997, 1998, 1999, 2001, 2005, 2007, 2009.

Vintage champagne (like vintage port) is made only in exceptional years, the best of late being 1990, 1995, 1996, 1998, 2002, 2004, 2008.

ageing

Ageing is the process by which wines settle down after fermentation, mature and improve, and nowhere do they do this better than in oak barrels.

Great differences are achieved by the size of the barrel, the type of oak used (usually French *Limousin, Allier* or *Tronçais*) and by whether it is old oak or new oak, or a mixture of the two. New oak contains vanillin, which leads wines that have been in oak for any length of time to smell of vanilla. Chardonnay is particularly well suited to

spending time in oak, by which process it takes on a deeper colour and fuller, softer, vanilla-like flavours. Indeed, it is extraordinary how much flavour Chardonnay does get from oak.

Some producers prefer not to use oak, because they feel that it imparts too much flavour to their wines, and so use stainless steel instead. Other producers feel that oak is essential whilst some even use oak chips as a rather unsatisfactory short cut method to imparting the unique flavour associated with oak.

white wine: quality classifications

Wine laws are very strict and their purpose is twofold: to protect the producer by ensuring that his region's reputation isn't undermined by the unscrupulous practices of some rogue producer, and to protect the consumer by guaranteeing the basic quality and character of the wine.

In general, France's stringent *Appellation d'Origine Contrôlée* (AOC) laws give a guarantee of a wine's origins and the authenticity of the grape variety, but without guaranteeing quality. The categories below AOC are *Vins Délimité de Qualité Supérieure* (VDQS), *Vin de Pays and Vin de Table*: these are for lower-quality wines and have less rigid production restrictions.

In Burgundy, a classification of *Premiers Crus* and *Grands Crus* identify the best vineyards, based on location; Alsace has elements of both systems.

Italy has a similar system, the *Denominazione di Origine Controllata* (DOC), although many top producers consider it too restrictive and make great wines which are obliged to be classified as

Vino da Tavola. A new classification, *Indicazione Geografica Tipica* (IGT) has been introduced to alleviate some of the confusion.

Germany's classifications of quality refer to the ripeness of the grapes and therefore to the sweetness of the wine.

Virtually every European wine-growing region has its own rules about which grapes may be used where and by what method they may be grown and vinified. Where they do not exist, individual producers may create a structure of their own.

Spain and Italy designate their wines *Reserva* or *Riserva* to indicate a certain period in oak, a treatment that is usually confined to only the best wines, unlike the French, whose categories relate to location.

New World wines are not subject to such strict restrictions – something that is often more than made up for by producers' giving extraordinarily detailed information on the back label.

white wine: storing & serving

Only a few white wines improve with age – for example, top-class white burgundy, Chablis, Sauternes and vintage champagne. Most white wine is likely to be for immediate consumption.

Store white wines as you would red wines, on their sides somewhere cool and dark and away from damp, vibration and strong smells. Wine racks are readily available and can be shaped to fit the most awkward spots. Alternatively, you can do a lot

worse than use a cardboard wine box lying on its side (if the bottles are stoppered with a cork).

White wine is best served chilled rather than ice cold; an hour in the fridge should be sufficient.

To open a champagne bottle, remove the foil and wire and hold the bottle at a slant with its base in your strong hand and the cork in the other hand. Hold the cork firmly while twisting the bottle

slowly; don't shake it. Ease the cork out gently covering it with your palm while ensuring that a glass is nearby in case the wine should froth out. Serve in tall glasses to preserve the bubbles that the winemaker has striven so hard to achieve.

Fill no more than a quarter of your glass and look at the wine, preferably against a white background. The wine should be clear and bright without any cloudiness or haziness. Holding the stem, swirl the glass around to release the bouquet. Take a good sniff; it should smell clean and fresh. Almost anything that might be wrong with a wine can be detected on the nose – by odours of mustiness, perhaps, or dampness.

Take a mouthful of the wine, drawing air into the mouth as you do so. Roll the liquid around your tongue and then spit or swallow. What is it like? Is it sweet or dry, light or full-bodied? Does it remind you of anything? The taste of a fine wine remains in the mouth, and its many components – its acidity, alcohol, fruit and tannin – should have combined so pleasantly that you want nothing more than to take another sip.

glossary

Acid/acidity Acids occur naturally in wine and are crucial in giving it character and structure and in helping it to age.

Aroma The varietal smell of a wine.

Balance A wine's harmonious combination of acids, tannins, alcohol, fruit and flavour.

Bereich (German) Term for a wine-producing district.

Bianco (Italian) White.

Blanc (French) White.

Blanc de blancs (French) A white wine made only from white grapes.

Blanc de noirs (French) A white wine made only from black (red) grapes.

Blanco (Spanish) White.

Blind tasting A tasting of wines at which the labels and shapes of the bottles are concealed from the tasters.

Bodega (Spanish) Winery.

Body The weight and structure of a wine.

Botrytis cinerea A fungus that, when it shrivels and rots white grapes, concentrates their flavours and sugars, leading to dessert wines that are high in alcohol and richness of flavour. It is also known as noble rot, *pourriture noble* and *edelfäule*.

Bouquet The complex scent of a wine that develops as it matures.

Cantina (Italian) Winery or cellar.

Carafe Simple decanter without a stopper.

Cave (French) Cellar.

Cellar book A useful way of noting what wines you have bought, from where and at what price, as well as recording when you consumed them and what they tasted like.

Cepa (Spanish) Term for vine variety.

Cépage (French) Term for vine variety.

Chai (French) Place for storing wine.

Chambrer From *chambre*, the French word for 'room', the practice of allowing a wine gradually to reach room temperature before drinking.

Château (French) Term for a wine-growing property – chiefly used in Bordeaux.

Claret Term given to the red wines of Bordeaux.

Climat (French) Burgundian term for a particular vineyard.

Clos (French) Enclosed vineyard.

Colheita (Portuguese) Vintage. A term also used for single-vintage ports.

Corkage Charge levied on customers in restaurants who bring in their own wine.

Corked Condition, indicated by a musty odour, where a wine is contaminated by a faulty cork.

Cosecha (Spanish) Vintage.

Côte (French) Hillside of vineyards.

Cradle A wicker basket in which some restaurants present a bottle of undecanted red wine – usually a burgundy – to the table.

Crémant (French) Semi-sparkling.

Cru (French) Growth or vineyard.

Cru Classé (French) Classed Growth, especially those 61 red wines of the Médoc (and one from the Graves) in Bordeaux that were graded into five categories determined by price (and therefore, in theory, quality) in 1855. Elsewhere in Bordeaux, similar classifications followed for the red wines of Graves in 1953 and for St Émilion in 1954 (revised in 1969 and 1985).

Cuvée (French) Blended or specially selected wine.

Decanter Glass container with a stopper into which red wines and ports are decanted in order to allow them to breathe or to remove them from their sediment.

Demi-sec (French) Semi-sweet.

Dolce (Italian) Sweet.

Domaine (French) Property or estate.

Doux (French) Sweet.

Dulce (Spanish) Sweet.

Fermentation The transformation of grape juice into wine, whereby yeasts - naturally present in grapes and occasionally added in cultured form - convert sugars into alcohol.

Fortified wine A wine - such as port, sherry, Madeira or Vin Doux Naturel - to which alcohol has been added, either in order to stop it fermenting before all its sugars are turned into alcohol (thus maintaining its sweetness) or simply to strengthen it.

Frizzante (Italian) Semi-sparkling.

Grand cru (French) Term used for top-quality wines in Alsace, Bordeaux, Burgundy and Champagne.

Halbtrocken (German) Medium dry.

Horizontal tasting A tasting of several different wines from the same vintage.

Jahrgang (German) Vintage.

Keller (German) Cellar.

Landwein (German) A level of quality wine just above simple table wine, equivalent to the French vin de pays.

Late harvest Very ripe grapes picked late when their sweetness is most concentrated.

Meritage Term first coined in 1988 for California wines blended from the classic red varieties of Bordeaux.

Méthode traditionelle The method - involving a secondary fermentation in bottle - by which champagnes and top-quality sparkling wines are made.

Moelleux (French) Sweet.

Mousse (French) The effervescence that froths in a glass of sparkling wine when it is poured, and which seems to wink at you.

Mousseux (French) Sparkling.

Négoçiant (French) Wine merchant, shipper or grower who buys wine or grapes in bulk from several sources before vinifying and/or bottling the wine himself.

Non-vintage (NV) Term applied to any wine that is a blend of two or more different vintages, notably champagne and port.

Nose The overall sense given off by a wine on being smelled. It is not just the wine's scent; the nose also conveys information about the wine's well-being.

Oak Much wine is aged in oak barrels, something which is typified by whiffs of vanilla or cedarwood.

Oxidized Term used to describe wine that has deteriorated owing to overlong exposure to air.

Perlant (French) A term that refers to a wine with the faintest of sparkles in it.

Perlwein (German) A type of low-grade semi-sparkling wine. Pétillant (French) Slightly sparkling.

Phylloxera An aphid-like insect that attacks the roots of vines with disastrous results.

Punt The indentation at the bottom of a bottle, serving not only to catch any sediment but also to strengthen the bottle.

Quinta (Portuguese) Wine-growing estate.

Récolte (French) Crop or vintage.

Rosso (Italian) Red.

Rouge (French) Red.

Sec (French) Dry.

Secco (Italian) Dry.

Seco (Spanish/Portuguese) Dry.

Sediment The deposit that forms after a wine has spent a lengthy period in the bottle.

Sekt (German) The German, not for dry - which is *trocken* - but for sparkling wine.

Sommelier Wine waiter.

Spittoon Receptacle into which wine is expectorated at a wine tasting.

Spritzer A refreshing drink made from white wine and soda or sparkling mineral water and usually served with ice.

Spumante (Italian) Sparkling.

Sur lie Term given to the process of ageing wines on their lees or sediment prior to bottling, resulting in a greater depth of flavour.

Tafelwein (German) Table wine.

Tannin The austere acid - and necessary preservative - found in some red wines, usually young ones, which derives from grape skins and stalks combined with the oak barrels in which the wine has been aged.

Tastevin A small silver tasting dish, most commonly used in Burgundy.

Terroir (French) Literally, 'soil' or 'earth', but the term also encompasses climate, drainage, position and anything that contributes to the mystery that makes one wine taste as it does while its immediate neighbours – grown and produced in the same way - taste different.

Tinto (Spanish/Portuguese) Red.

Trocken (German) Dry.

Ullage The amount of air in a bottle or barrel between the top of the wine and the bottom of the cork or bung.

Varietal A wine named after the grape (or its major constituent grape) from which it is made. Variety Term for each distinctive breed of grape.

Vendange (French) Harvest or vintage.

Vendange tardive (French) Late harvest.

Vendemmia (Italian) Harvest or vintage.

Vendimia (Spanish) Harvest or vintage.

Vertical tasting A tasting of several wines from the same property that all come from different vintages.

Vigneron (French) Wine grower.

Vin de pays (French) Country wine of a level higher than table wine.

Vin de table (French) Table wine.

Vin Doux Naturel (VDN) (French) A fortified wine that has been sweetened and strengthened by the addition of alcohol, either before or after fermentation has taken place.

Vin ordinaire (French) Basic wine not subject to any regulations.

Vinification Wine making.

Vino da tavola (Italian) Table wine.

Vino de mesa (Spanish) Table wine.

Vintage Both the year of the actual grape harvest as well as the wine made from those grapes.

Viticulture Cultivation of grapes.

Weight The body and/or strength of a wine.

index

acknowledgments

I would like to thank Anne Ryland for coming up with idea, and Alison Starling, Gabriella Le Grazie, Luis Peral-Aranda and Maddalena Bastianelli for making the project such an enjoyable one. I am also most grateful to Judith Murray, to David Roberts MW and to Alan Williams for his beautiful photographs, some of which were taken at Villandry and Berry Bros and Rudd Ltd, to whom also many thanks. Finally, of course, I would like to thank my wife Marina, ever patient and ever wise, and without whom . . .

Villandry
170 Great Portland Street
London W1N 5TB, UK
+ 44 (0)20 7631 3131
www.villandry.com

Berry Bros & Rudd Ltd
3 St James's Street
London SW1A 1EG, UK
+ 44 (0)870 900 4300
www.bbr.com

The author and publisher would also like to thank the following companies for allowing us to photograph their vineyards, wineries and cellars:

AUSTRALIA
Barossa Valley, South Australia
d'Arenberg, McLaren Vale, South Australia
Rockford Vineyards, Barossa Valley, South Australia

CALIFORNIA
Beringer Wine Estates, St Helena, Napa Valley
De Loach Vineyards, Sonoma Valley
Heitz Wine Cellars, St Helena, Napa Valley
Schramsberg Vineyards, Napa Valley